LOVE POEMS OF CATULLUS

T0022993

LOVE POEMS OF CATULLUS

Gaius Valerius Catullus

edited by Tynan Kogane

A New Directions Paperbook

Manufactured in the United States of America
First published as a New Directions Paperbook in 2023
Design by Marian Bantjes

Library of Congress Cataloging-in-Publication Data
Names: Catullus, Gaius Valerius, author. | Kogane, Tynan, 1985– editor.
Title: The love poems of Catullus / Gaius Valerius Catullus ;
edited by Tynan Kogane.
Description: New York : New Directions Publishing Corporation, [2023]
Identifiers: LCCN 2023016493 | ISBN 9780811237499
(paperback ; acid-free paper)
Subjects: LCSH: Catullus, Gaius Valerius—Translations into English. |
Love poetry, Latin—Translations into English. | LCGFT: Love poetry.
Classification: LCC PA6275.E5 K64 2023 | DDC 874/.01—dc23/eng/20230503
LC record available at https://lccn.loc.gov/2023016493

10 9 8 7 6 5 4 3 2 1

New Directions Books are published for James Laughlin
by New Directions Publishing Corporation
80 Eighth Avenue, New York 10011

TABLE OF CONTENTS

✞   7

I   To whom do I give this pleasant new little
          book,
     just now polished with dry pumice?
     To you, Cornelius; for you used
     to think my trifles were something,
     even then when you alone of the Italians
     dared to explain all history in three books,
     learned, by Jupiter, and worked through!
     Wherefore, take for yourself this book,
          whatever it is,
     such as it is, and may it, o patron maiden,
     remain lasting for more than one generation.

Translated by Vincent Katz

2   Sparrow my lover's delight,
     playing then holding on tight
     to her finger, and pecking at corn,
     beak pecking her flesh like a thorn,
     I'd prefer that I could make her smile
     and lighten her gloom for a while
     like you do. But at least she has you
     and for now that will just have to do.

Translated by Roz Kaveney

2   Sparrow, my girl's pleasure, delight of my girl,
a thing to delude her, her secret darling
whom she offers her fingernail to peck at,
teasing unremittingly your sharp bite,
when desire overcomes her, shining with love
my dear, I do not know what longing takes her,
I think, it is the crest of passion quieted
gives way to this small solace against sorrow,
could I but lose myself with you as she does,
breathe with a light heart, be rid of these cares!

Translated by Louis & Celia Zukofsky

2   (My Lady's Pet)

Catullus observes his love and her pet at play

On her lap one of the matted terriers.
She was combing around its genitals.
It grinned I grinned back.
It's the one she calls *Little Bottle* after Deng
    Xiaoping.

Translated by Anne Carson

On Catullus 2

I think when
passion dies
it'd be good to play
I don't know what
with my bright love
if only I could
play with you too
like she does

By Bernadette Mayer

3   (For Trent, on the Death of His Pet
        Dove, Larry)

Weep, Venuses & Cupids—vent,
All gentle folk with human feeling—
Trent's bird has died and left him reeling—
That bird was everything to Trent.

It was denominated Larry,
Christened thus, for deemed a boy—
Until *she* laid an egg—then joy!
A ring-necked dove, no mere canary,

Two years she shared his smiles and sorrows,
He fed her treats and changed her papers,
Now let us weep, and light the tapers,
For Larry has no more tomorrows;

Now she has flown the loathsome road
Down which all mortal men must troop
And not return. She's flown the coop
And found a dusty new abode.

The cat was ruled as cause of death—
I see its eyes, like wicked lamps

As round as innocence; it vamps
In the black ground of a Velásquez,

But wrongful Death, it's you I blame.
You petty thief, it was absurd
To pilfer such a dainty bird
With so incongruous a name.

Greedy for everything that's fluffy,
You pocket all that's soft and sweet—
And make your villainy complete
By leaving Trent's eyes red and puffy.

Translated by A. E. Stallings

On Catullus 3

From A Letter From Lesbia

... So, praise the gods, Catullus is away!
And let me tend you this advice, my dear:
Take any lover that you will, or may,
Except a poet. All of them are queer.

It's just the same—a quarrel or a kiss
Is but a tune to play upon his pipe.
He's always hymning that or wailing this;
Myself, I much prefer the business type.

That thing he wrote, the time the sparrow
    died—
(Oh, most unpleasant—gloomy, tedious
    words!)
I called it sweet, and made believe I cried;
The stupid fool! I've always hated birds ...

By Dorothy Parker

5   Let us live, my Lesbia, and let us love each
          other,
     caring nothing for what jealous old men may
          say about us.
     Suns set and then they rise again,
     but when our sun sets, that brief light, there
          will be only a perpetual night of slumber.
     Give me a thousand kisses, and a hundred
          more,
     another thousand and a second hundred,
     then another thousand and another hundred.
     And when we have kissed many thousand times
     we will lose count but go on kissing
     so that no one with the evil eye
     can hurt us or stop our endless lovemaking.

Translated by James Laughlin

5   Live love Lesbia you and I together
staunch stayed stolid thoughts you and I must
      never
take tight to our hearts but recall in sorrow
one sun sets today one will rise tomorrow
our bright splendid light once gone goes
      forever
that night when it comes you and I must
      weather
come kiss hold me tight let me hear your
      laughter
come now fifty more and a hundred after
then when we have done all I am intending
that kiss will become one embrace unending
all small minded men cannot wreck confusion
nor for all our love can brake our illusion

Translated by Samuel R. Delany

5   (To Ellen)

Oh! might I kiss those eyes of fire,
A million scarce would quench desire:
Still would I steep my lips in bliss,
And dwell an age on every kiss:
Nor then my soul should sated be,
Still would I kiss and cling to thee:
Nought should my kiss from thine dissever,
Still would we kiss and kiss for ever:
E'en though the numbers did exceed
The yellow harvest's countless seed:
To part would be a vain endeavour:
Could I desist? ah! never—never!

Translated by Lord Byron

5   Let's live Catullus, or else let us love—
     One or the other, though rumour now
     Lets live and love till the sun goes out.
     The daylight lasts too long for us
     Who follow after our wills' distortion
     Along forevers of chosen darkness.

     Those lovers were simple as fire but we
     Advance into ice; they melted like rivers
     But we are others; pale northman,
     Resist that sun that shall offend you;
     Be dumb, though time upon time I call
     Catulle to the ancient stones or sing
     These epithalamia always arrested.

Translated by Muriel Spark

(The Passionate Shepherd to his Love)

Come live with me and be my love,
And we will all the pleasures prove
That hills and valleys, dales and fields,
Woods or steepy mountain yields.

And we will sit upon the rocks,
Seeing the shepherds feed their flocks
By shallow rivers, to whose falls
Melodious birds sing madrigals.

And I will make thee beds of roses
And a thousand fragrant posies,
A cap of flowers, and a kirtle
Embroidered all with leaves of myrtle;

A gown made of the finest wool,
Which from our pretty lambs we pull;
Fair-lined slippers for the cold,
With buckles of the purest gold;

A belt of straw and ivy-buds,
With coral clasps and amber studs:

And if these pleasures may thee move,
Come live with me and be my love.

The shepherd swains shall dance and sing
For thy delight each May morning:
If these delights thy mind may move,
Then live with me and be my love.

By Christopher Marlowe

7   You ask how many of your kisses,
     Lesbia, would be enough for me and more?
     However great the number of Libyan sands
     that lie around silphium-rich Cyrene
     between the oracle of burning Jove
     and the sacred sepulcher of ancient Battus;
     or however many stars, when night is silent,
     witness the furtive trysts of men;
     that you kiss so many kisses
     is enough and more for maddened Catullus;
     may the curious be unable to count them
     or to bind with evil tongue.

Translated by Vincent Katz

7   Kiss me, sweet: the wary lover
    Can your favours keep, and cover,
    When the common courting jay
    All your bounties will betray.
    Kiss again! no creature comes;
    Kiss, and score up wealthy sums
    On my lips, thus hardly sundered,
    While you breathe. First give a hundred,
    Then a thousand, then another
    Hundred, then unto the other
    Add a thousand, and so more:
    Till you equal with the store,
    All the grass that Rumney yields,
    Or the sands in Chelsea fields,
    Or the drops in silver Thames,
    Or the stars that gild his streams,
    In the silent Summer-nights,
    When youths ply their stolen delights;
    That the curious may not know
    How to tell 'em as they flow,
    And the envious, when they find
    What their number is, be pined.

                              Translated by Ben Jonson

8   You had better stop playing the fool, Catullus,
     And accept that what you see is lost, is lost.
     Once your days were shining
     When you used to go wherever the girl led you,
     She loved as none will ever be loved.
     Then those many pleasant things were done
     Which you wanted and the girl was willing to
          do;
     Certainly then your days were shining.
     She wants those things no more: you had better
          not want them,
     Nor ask for what will not be given, nor live in
          pain.
     Be patient, harden your mind.
     Good-bye, girl. Already Catullus is hardened.
     He does not seek you, and will not, since you
          are unwilling.
     But you will suffer when you are asked for
          nothing at night.
     It is the end. What life remains for you?
     Who now will come to you? Who will think
          you pretty?
     Whom will you now love? Whose will say you
          are?

Whom will you kiss? And whose lips will you
    bite?
But you, Catullus, accept fate and be firm.

Translated by C. H. Sisson

II   You, Hate and Love, companions of this poet
      Where cities of fire sustain me, and where
      The glaciers clash together the northern
          tundras'
          Assaulted waters,

      Shall face these weathers of my instruction.
      Then travel courageously, notorious couriers
      Into the icelock, and beyond its zero
          Seek out my love.

      Remind him first of all how he survives
      The flower of death blown over that
          relinquished
      Meadow where lover and plough break
          Lover and flower alike.

      But let him not believe that a winter invoked
      Can blight the bespoken summers nor silence
          him
      Being that one who called time upon time,
          Lesbia to the ancient stones.

                              Translated by Muriel Spark

II   Furius and Aurelius, aides to Catullus,
Whether he penetrate the ultimate Indies
Where the rolling surf on the shores of
      morning
         Beats and again beats:

Or in the land of bedouin, the soft Arabs,
Or Parthians, the ungentlemanly archers,
Or where the Nile with seven similar
      streamlets
         Colors the clear sea;

Or if he cross the loftier Alpine passes
And view the monuments of almighty Caesar,
The Rhine, and France, and even those
      remotest
         Shuddersome British—

Friends, prepared for all of these, whatever
Province the celestial ones may wish me—
Take a little bulletin to my mistress,
      Unpleasantly worded:

Let her live and thrive with her fornicators
Of whom she hugs three hundred in an
    evening,
With no true love for any, leaving them
    broken-
      Winded the same way.

She need not, as in the old days, look for my
    love.
By her own fault it died, like a fallen flower
At the field's edge, after the passing harrow
      Touched it and left it.

Translated by Robert Fitzgerald

13   Tomorrow night, or the night after,
My friend, godwilling, you shall dine
In style *chez moi*—that's if you bring
A sumptuous meal—and bring some wine,
And don't forget a pretty gal,
A pinch of wit and all the laughter.
You'll dine at my place like a king,
Prince charming! I say, that is if
You bring it—the pocket of your pal
Is full of cobwebs. But I propose
In turn I'll pour the love out neat,
And give an even finer treat,
My girl's perfume—not off the shelf,
A gift from Venus and Love himself!
I promise once you get a whiff
You'll pray to be just one big nose.

Translated by A. E. Stallings

15   I want you to take care of my boy friend,
Aurelius. All I ask is one simple favor,
that, if in your heart you ever desired
to preserve one thing clean and undefiled,
you'll keep the kid nice and pure for me.
I don't mean from others, I'm not afraid
of those folks out there in the streets
walking around minding their own business,
it's you, and your prick, the polluter
of good and bad boys both, that scares me.
Now you can go whip it out and use it
whenever you want, on anyone or anything,
except for this kid, that's all I ask.
But, if you're just plain stupid, or go
crazy enough to try it, you back-stabbing
son of a bitch, then I weep for you now,
ankles bound, bare-assed, gate wide open,
with catfish and carrots rammed up your hole.

Translated by Carl Sesar

16 All right I'll bugger you and suck your pricks,
    Aurelius and Furius, you pair of sodomites
    Who imagine, on the strength of my verses,
    That I am lacking in reserve as they are.
    But although the sacred poet ought to be chaste
    It does not follow that his verses should be.

Translated by C. H. Sisson

31   (Catullus recollected)

Dear little Sirmio
Of all capes and islands
Wherever Neptune rides the coastal waters and
    the open sea
You really are the nicest.

How glad I am to see you again, how fondly I
    look at you.

No sooner had I left Bithynia—and what was
    the name of the other place?
And was safely at sea
I thought only of seeing you.

Really is anything nicer
After working hard and being thoroughly
    worried
Than to leave it all behind and set out for home
Dear old home and one's comfortable bed?

Even if one wears oneself out paying for them.

Translated by Stevie Smith

32   Ipsitilla, my sweet, dear girl,
      Little furnace, send word at once,
      Please, that I may spend the
      Afternoon with you. And if I may,
      Be sure no other cocks are let
      Into your henhouse. And don't
      You go walking the streets;
      Stay home and have ready for me
      Nine of your nicest continuous
      Fucks. (And don't forget the
      Wine.) May I come as soon as
      Possible? I've had my lunch
      But I'm hot for it and my
      Prick is trying to poke holes
      In my shirt and the blanket.

Translated by James Laughlin

33   (Hendecasyllables on Catullus 33)

You have the balls to say you will be with me
but you hardly ever are, then you say you're
    scared
of your parents' opinion, they pay your rent
I wouldn't mind that if they didn't think I
was a whore ridden with AIDS disease & worse
    things
but I am I and my little dog knows me
in the most astonishingly bourgeois way
I even pay my self-employment tax now
and put leftovers into expensive tinfoil
to be used in imaginable tomorrows
therefore I protest my bad reputation
but I do wander all night in my vision

By Bernadette Mayer

35   Dear papyrus, please tell
        My friend Caecilius the love poet
        To leave behind the buildings of New Como
        And beaches of Larius and come to Verona.
        I want him to hear some thoughts from
        A mutual friend of ours.
        If he's sensible, he'll eat up the road,
        Although the shining girl may summon him
              back
        A thousand times as he goes, and throw
        Both arms around his neck, and beg him to
              linger.
        For if my report is true, she
        Is undone by the strength of her love for him.
        For as soon as she read his unfinished
        Mistress of Dindymus, fires of passion
        Coursed the inner paths of the poor girl's
              marrow.
        And I don't blame you—you're more learned
        A girl than the Sapphic Muse; for it is
              charmingly
        Unfinished, Caecilius' Great Mother.

                            Translated by Daisy Dunn

37   Less pub than brothel, and you, the regulars
     The ninth pillar from Castor and Pollux,
     Do you think you are the only ones equipped
          with a penis,
     That you are the only ones licensed for fucking
     And that the rest who do it are merely goats?
     Do you think, as you sit waiting in rows
     A hundred or two hundred together, that I
          shall not dare
     To do the whole lot of you, two hundred
          together?
     Think again: I will draw scorpions
     All over the walls of the place.
     For my girl, who has escaped from my arms,
     Who was loved as much, and more than any is
          loved,
     For whom I have expended all my forces,
     She is there. You, the great and the good, all
          love her,
     You the valueless, corrupt, adulterous all love
          her;
     You above all Egnatius
     Long-haired son of a rabbit-toothed
          Celtiberian,

Only made good by your beard
Your teeth whitened by Spanish piss.

Translated by C. H. Sisson

43   All Hail; young lady with a nose
      by no means too small,
      With a foot unbeautiful,
      and with eyes that are not black,
      With fingers that are not long, and with a
            mouth undry,
      And with a tongue by no means too elegant,
      You are the friend of Formianus, the vendor of
            cosmetics,
      And they call you beautiful in the province,
      And you are even compared to Lesbia.

      O most unfortunate age!

Translated by Ezra Pound

43   (Hello Not Very Small Nosed Girl)

Catullus compares an unnamed girl to his own love.

Your nose is wrong.
Your feet are wrong.
Your eyes are wrong your mouth is wrong.
Your pimp is wrong even his name is wrong.
Who cares what they say, you're not—
Why can't I
Live in the nineteenth century.

Translated by Anne Carson

43   (After Catullus, 43)

Hi there, dear sister, I'm sad
But here to tell you
That you never did amount to anything
Facial expressions just like your mother
Nose by no means tiny
Married a couple of people
So now you sit in a house
Cleaning or not cleaning a window
Newsflash: no one cares about time
But you do it like it's so moral being punctual
Truly an actress, but you poorly acted the part
Of someone who isn't crazy
No I can't say your ankles *are* fat
But dear lady, who would have had your ass
Except now I do
Seemingly connected we are, in the worst way
And so I must tell you
You are a no good person
A criminal, really, a scoundrel
No, really, a liar
He said the person was cold, maybe a bit
    disdainful
I said, welcome to my life

You know some people like history
Or want to make history
But I am history
If you would have fucked me
I would have been OK being Plath
But instead I'm Sexton
If somebody asks me what I like
It's not food or sex
It's looking at things and being in love
Not sure what of this you did offer me
Never did amount to anything
So with this
I go

Translated by Dorothea Lasky

45   Septimius with his arms entwined round his
       Acme
    says: my dear, if I do not love to destruction
    down the long road to hell and love but you
       forever,
    may I wander lonely through India, Africa,
    and be discovered, naked, by a green-eyed,
       ravenous lion.

    As he spoke, Love sneezed, an omen of good
       fortune.

    Then Acme, head thrown back, her eyes, her
       fluid body
    drunken with love, her rose-red lips to his
       replying:
    here's my life, Septimius. I swear to serve my
       lord till
    flames of love consume me, now flowing
       through my veins and
    melting me. The core of my being turns to fire.

    Love sneezed again and they received his own,
       his sacred blessing.

Under his wings, they marched forth, love for
     love, united,
blood fused in a rich liquid.

Septimius, a poor young man, finds more
     wealth in his Acme
than all the gold of Britain and the mines of
     Syria.
He is her life. His arms alone hold pleasure for
     sweet Acme.
Is there good fortune on this earth equal to his
     treasure;
who shall see again and know greater love than
     theirs is?

Translated by Horace Gregory

48   I'd kiss your eyes three hundred thousand times
         If you would let me, Juventius, kiss them
         All the time, your darling eyes, eyes of honey
         And even if the formal field of kissing
         Had more kisses than there's corn in August's
             fields
         I still wouldn't have had enough of you

Translated by Bernadette Mayer

48   Your honeyed eyes, Juventius,
       If you would let one kiss,
       Three hundred thousand would to us
       Seem nothing much amiss:
       Could all earth's ears of corn eclipse
       That heavenly harvest of the lips?

Translated by Arthur Symons

48   Juventius if you let me
      go on kissing your honey-

      ed eyes I'd kiss them
      three hundred thousand

      times and that might not
      be enough if it were

      less than all the ripe
      corn of the harvest.

Translated by James Laughlin

50 (Yesterday Licinius at Our Ease)

Catullus addresses Licinius with affection.

I guess around sunset we started to drink.
And lay on the floor writing lines
For songs that cold
Night smell coming in
The window I left about four went
Home.
Opened the fridge.
Closed it lay down got up.
Lay down.
Lay.
Turned.
Not morning yet.
I just want to talk to you.
Why does love happen?
So then I grew old and died and wrote this.
Be careful it's worldsharp.

Translated by Anne Carson

50   Yesterday, Licinius, we played a lot
      at leisure on my writing tablets,
      as we'd decided to be alluring.
      Each of us writing little verses
      was playing with meter, now this one, now that,
      repaying line for line through laughter and wine.
      And I went away from that place burning
      with your charm, Licinius, and your wit,
      so that food was no solace to me in my misery,
      nor would sleep close my eyes with rest,
      but untamed in a frenzy I was tossed on the
            entire
      bed, desiring to see daybreak,
      so that I might speak with you at once and be
            with you.
      But after my limbs, exhausted from labor,
      lay down half-dead on the couch,
      I composed this poem for you, my delight,
      from which you may perceive my unhappiness.
      Beware of being proud, and beware of spitting
      upon my prayers, I beg you, my little gem,
      lest Nemesis demand punishments from you in
            return.
      She is a violent goddess: don't offend her.

                                    Translated by Vincent Katz

51   He's like a god, the guy who sits across
From you—a god. Is that all right to say?
He gazes at you while I'm at a loss,
He listens to the play

Of music in your laugh. But me, poor dolt,
I'm stunned speechless, sweetheart; just a
     glance
Leaves my wits reeling, senses in revolt;
I haven't got a chance:

My tongue thickens, a fever starts to spike
Under my skin, a white noise seems to block
My ears, my eyes go double blind. It's like
Anaphylactic shock.

Catullus, time's your trouble, too much time,
The leisure you wallowed in. And at what cost!
Leisure has brought down kings; and in their
     prime
Whole cities have been lost.

Translated by A. E. Stallings

From 51 (To Constantia Singing)

My brain is wild, my breath comes quick—
The blood is listening in my frame,
And thronging shadows, fast and thick,
Fall on my overflowing eyes:
My heart is quivering like a flame;
As morning dew, that in the sunbeam dies,
I am dissolved in these consuming ecstasies.

Translated by Percy Bysshe Shelley

51   (Clodia)

e.g., we are the only two in town who
smoke these cigarettes. I cannot learn too
     much
of her. Like migraine: fascinating, hurtful,
larger than oneself.

How does hate swing through fixation into
     love,
or something like? So if she drives past in the
family car I want to part the traffic
like a sea for her—

which is confusing, at the very least. She
stirs some belly-bowl of kindness not quite
     mine.
How many indiscretions does she know of?
Every one, of course;

and Sunday afternoon means she's across town
with the children, all the family to lunch.
The banter flies. I scrub the cooker, wash
     clothes,
keep a life ticking.

A late wasp guns its engine at my window.
It is dark before I let it out to face
a firing-squad of stars. And nothing quite puts
distance like the stars.

Her husband left me green with want, she
        knows that.
But I'm sick for something further back. Look:
        I'm
the stickyfingered brat still clamouring at
the apron, whining.

Translated by Tiffany Atkinson

58   Caelius! My Lesbia, that one
      That one Catullus loved
      More than a self
      Who now is in the portals
      She peels the skins off
      Remus's particular sons

Translated by Dorothea Lasky

58 Caelius, Lesbia new star, Lesbia a light,
    all light, Lesbia, whom Catullus (o name
    loss) whom his eyes caught so as avid of none,
    none else—slunk in the driveways, the dingy
        parts
    glut magnanimous Remus, his knee-high pots.

Translated by Louis & Celia Zukofsky

From 61 (Rubbing Dry Sticks)

Eros has broken his bow,
He has had to send it to the shop
For repairs, but he's still
Starting conflagrations of the heart
By rubbing dry sticks together.
Who here in the village
Would have dreamed it possible
That those two could have become
What the gossip columnist of the
Goshen Star calls an "item"
Lump-faced Louella who's retired
From teaching social sciences
In the grade school; she received
A medal from the State Department
Of Education for forty years
Of devoted service. And bibulous Bob
Who never kept a job for more
Than a year but everybody loves him.
Now he lives on welfare. Eros smiles
Io Hymen ... Hymenaeus Io!
It's a happy sight to see the two
Antique lovers strolling hand in hand
Along the village street, not to

The bar, love has put Bob on the
Wagon, but to the pizza parlor.
Io Hymen ... Hymenaeus Io!
Their wedding has been announced.
Our beloved First Selectman will
Preside at the ceremony in the
Town Hall. Everyone in the village
Will come to wish them well.
Io Hymen ... Hymenaeus Io!
Will Eros be hiding in the back
Of the room scanning the faces
For his next triumph?

Translated by James Laughlin

67 CATULLUS:
O sweet delightful delightful door, a pleasure
    to the husband and to the husband's father,
    bliss for all parents
who have penises
Be in good health my door, hello to you, let
    Jupiter
or God increase your self's good works
Door who serviced Balbus well and once upon
    a time
While he still held his own old seat in the
    home,
that is, he lived
And to what extent, how much, do you bring
    bear carry
back and backwards to swim to stream to slow
    to serve
so badly
After the stretched out fact of the married man
    versus
the dead man
In the old sleepy house to have been so
    abandoned ...
Why have you become so changed to us?

DOOR:
So it please, Caecilius, son of Balbus,
whom I now serve, I haven't changed
nor is it my fault: it never was
No matter what anybody says
I've committed no sin
People will always blame the door
whenever a bad thing happens
Well, let them talk: I didn't

CATULLUS:
It's not enough for you to speak one word
    about that but
to do it so anyone can sense it and feel it and
    see it

DOOR:
How can I? Nobody wants to know the truth

CATULLUS:
Well that's what we wish for: you have to tell us
things without a doubt

DOOR:
Well, first of all, she wasn't a virgin
when she came to us
It was old Balbus himself who had her first
because his poor son's limp dagger hung
like a withered beet that never even reached
mid-tunic; yes, it was the father got in the
    marriage bed
and defiled it
whether from pure lust
or simply the urge to do his son's work:
somebody had to do the proper thing
and undo a married virgin

CATULLUS:
He sure was one extremely high frequency
    father-in-law—
you speak too well of him—this parent pissed
    on the lap of
the wife of his son or maybe he pissed in her
    belly or maybe
he pissed on her breasts or maybe he pissed in
    a holy way
on his sons possession of his wife

DOOR:
Catullus, that's not all they say,
and not just in Verona,
but throughout all of Brixia,
amata mater meae,
along Chinea's watchtower
wherever the river Mella flows
everybody knows
she's done it with
Postumius and Cornelius

CATULLUS:
Now here someone will say, What? Door! How
      did you know
all about us without ever leaving the threshold?
      Without
hearing people talking in secret away from you?
      Aren't
you just fixed under a small beam to shut and
      close as
much as usual and to open and expose what's
      going on
in the domicile?

DOOR:
I don't have to walk
I can hear her talk in a low voice
about all she does to her maids
She's not aware I have eyes and ears
I could mention one gentleman by name but I
    won't
though I can tell you he is tall
without lifting his red eyebrows
He was in court lately defending himself
but the pregnancy was false.

Translated by Bernadette Mayer (with Don Yorty)

70   (No One She Says)

Catullus wonders about lovers' oaths.

No one but you she says she swore.
Why one night a god threw open the door.
I loved you more.
River.
River.
River.
River.
River.
River.
River.
River   river   river   river   river   river   river.

Translated by Anne Carson

70 My love says that she would rather be
    in my bed than in Jupiter's, but we
    know that hot passion makes all women say
    words carved in water and then washed away.

Translated by Roz Kaveney

72   There was a time you said you knew only
     Catullus,
> Lesbia, that you wouldn't want to hold
> Jupiter over me.
I loved you then not just as a man loves his
girlfriend,
> But as a father loves his sons and sons-in-
> law.
Now I have got to know you. So even if I burn
more deeply
> You are still much cheaper and less
> significant to me.
How can that be, you say? Because such a
wound compels a lover
> To love more, but to like less.

Translated by Daisy Dunn

72   (Sonnet CL)

O, from what power hast thou this powerful
    might
With insufficiency my heart to sway?
To make me give the lie to my true sight,
And swear that brightness doth not grace the
    day?
Whence hast thou this becoming of things ill,
That in the very refuse of thy deeds
There is such strength and warrantise of skill
That, in my mind, thy worst all best exceeds?
Who taught thee how to make me love thee
    more,
The more I hear and see just cause of hate?
O, though I love what others do abhor,
With others thou shouldst not abhor my state:
    If thy unworthiness raised love in me,
    More worthy I to be beloved of thee.

By William Shakespeare

75   Now my mind's been brought to such a state—
and it's your fault,
> Lesbia!—been so skewed by its devotion
> to you,
I couldn't like you again, if you turned truest of
women;
> Yet couldn't fall out of love, not for the
> worst you could do.

Translated by John Frederick Nims

75   (To This Point Is My Mind Reduced)

Catullus is brought low.

Decay flaps upward from my mind O my love.
Where it fingers your crime.
The autumn night comes on so cool.

Translated by Anne Carson

76 (If for a Man Recalling Prior Benefactions)

Catullus reflects on his own piety.

Before my holy stoning in the wet kisses and
    the smell of sperm
I drove an ambulance for the Red Cross.
Do you think a man can be naturally pure?
In those days I kept a diary it fell out of my
    pocket the night
I carried you to the forge in my arms.
You grew freer and brighter with every stroke
    of the hammer.

Translated by Anne Carson

78a   It bothers me that a sweet girl's sweet lips
        got smeared all over with your slimy drool.
        But you'll pay: people will get wise to what
        you are, and pass the word on down through
            the ages.

Translated by Carl Sesar

79   Lesbius is beautiful. And why? Lesbia loves
           him.
       Loves him more than you and your family,
           Catullus,
       for he is the flower of an ancient lineage.

       Since he is delicate, refined, he'd sell your
           relatives
       and you, my dear Catullus,
       as slaves to buy the kisses of three boys if
           they've the courage
       to taste his vile saliva.

Translated by Horace Gregory

82   Quintius, if you want Catullus to owe his eyes
              to you,
        Or if there is something dearer than one's eyes,
        Don't rip from him what is much dearer to him
        Than his eyes or whatever is dearer than his
              eyes.

Translated by Vincent Katz

82   Quintius, if you want me to owe you my life
      or whatever more than my life I might care for,
      don't tear me away from what I care for even
      more than my life, yes, even more than my life.

Translated by Carl Sesar

83   Lesbia speaks evil of me with her husband near
            and he (damned idiot) loves to hear her.
      Chuckling, the fool is happy, seeing nothing,
            understanding nothing
      If she forgetting me fell silent, her heart would
            be his alone, content and peaceful;
      but she raves, spitting hatred upon me, all of
            which carries this meaning:
      I am never out of her mind, and what is more,
            she rises in fury against me
      with words that make her burn, her blood
            passionate for me.

Translated by Horace Gregory

83   Lesbia speaks evil
    To a man
    About me
    Igniting his sagging jollies
    You jackass
    You know nothing
    If her mind were quiet
    And clear of me
    She would say little
    Instead she fumes
    Over me
    She burns for me

Translated by Dorothea Lasky

85   I hate and love. Why? You may ask but
     It beats me. I feel it done to me, and ache.

Translated by Ezra Pound

85   Hate: and I love. Who knows why?
     Nothing I say chokes the ache.

Translated by Cid Corman

86   Quintia is beautiful to many, to me she's
        glowing, tall,
    Statuesque. These singular qualities I admit.
    That the ensemble is beautiful I deny: for there
        is no grace,
    No spark of wit in all that great body.
    Lesbia is beautiful, who alone, since she is the
        prettiest in toto,
    Has stolen all the charm from all the others.

Translated by Vincent Katz

86   (Quintia Is Beautiful to Many)

Catullus compares a certain Quintia to his own love.

There was a whiteness in you.
That kitten washed in another world look.
Good strong handshake for a girl but.
But.

Translated by Anne Carson

87   No woman, if she is honest, can say that she's
been blessed with greater love, my Lesbia,
than I have given you;
nor has any man held to a contract made
with more fidelity
than I have shown, my dear,
in loving you.

Translated by Horace Gregory

87   (Love's Infiniteness)

If yet I have not all thy love,
Deare, I shall never have it all.
I cannot breathe one other sigh, to move,
Nor can intreat one other teare to fall,
And all my treasure, which should purchase
    thee,
Sighs, teares, and oathes, and letters I have
    spent.

Translated by John Donne

87   No woman can say she was so much loved as
            you were,
      Lesbia my darling, no one has loved as I have;
      No trust was ever kept with such faith before
      As, on my side, my love for you was kept.

Translated by C. H. Sisson

91   I really was an idiot to trust
     someone I know to be obsessed with sin
     around my love. I thought, she's not his kin
     and so she's not a target for his lust.
     I'm mad for love of her, that's my excuse.
     So mad I somehow thought that she'd be safe,
     forgot he's one whom all restrictions chafe,
     thought he was bound by friendship who's so
          loose
     normal considerations don't apply.
     I burn for her with such intense desire,
     my commonsense consumed in raging fire.
     He reassured me, did not even lie.
     "I love her like a sister." Should have known
     that meant she's on his list of girls to bone.

Translated by Roz Kaveney

92   Always, getting on my nerves,
      always, making me look like a fool.
      For all that, all her stubborn chatter,
      the woman loves me.
      How do I know? Well, I see
      that I do
              exactly the same
                        myself:
      I damn her, with all my heart,
      yet, for the life of me, I love her.

Translated by Cid Corman

96   If anything can pierce impenetrable earth and
            echo in the silence
      of the grave, my Calvus, it is our sad memory
      of those we love. (Our longing for them makes
            them bloom again,
      quickened with love and friendship,
      even though they left us long ago, heavy with
            tears).
      Surely, your Quintilia now no longer cries
            against powerful death
      (who had taken her away from you too soon
            and she was gone).
      Look she is radiant, fixed in your mind, happy
            forever.

Translated by Horace Gregory

96   (Sonnet XXX)

When to the sessions of sweet silent thought
I summon up remembrance of things past,
I sigh the lack of many a thing I sought,
And with old woes new wail my dear time's
    waste:
Then can I drown an eye, unused to flow,
For precious friends hid in death's dateless
    night,
And weep afresh love's long since cancell'd woe,
And moan the expense of many a vanish'd
    sight:
Then can I grieve at grievances foregone,
And heavily from woe to woe tell o'er
The sad account of fore-bemoaned moan,
Which I new pay as if not paid before.
    But if the while I think on thee, dear friend,
    All losses are restored and sorrows end.

Translated by William Shakespeare

99   Honey while you played I stole
       a little kiss, Juventius, sweet sweet

       This didn't go unpunished & from then I'm
           fixed
       on the highest tearless crucifix
       I make myself clear with my tears
       it doesn't work and you're still mad

       Once when we kissed you used your spit
       to wipe your lips, oh your soft fingers
       you looked like you thought you might get
           AIDS
       from the dirty kiss of this diseased whore

       How come you always bring me love without
           rest
       It's all misery, you always torture me
       that small kiss was the bitterest

       And all you've given me since are punishments
       handed out like medicines for miserable love
       I'll never steal another kiss

                       Translated by Bernadette Mayer

100　Caelius burns for Aufilenus
　　　Quintius burns for Aufilena
　　　The blossom of Verona
　　　The brother and the sister
　　　Deified with the very sweet drink
　　　Of a secret brotherhood

　　　Which is preferable to favor?
　　　Oh it's you, Caelius
　　　You proved your worth
　　　When the numbing fire
　　　Hardened me

　　　Be content, Caelius
　　　Be mighty in love

Translated by Dorothea Lasky

104　How can I curse my love, the one I prize
　　　above all else, dearer than my own eyes?
　　　One harsh vile word? One syllable thereof?
　　　I can't; I am so deeply lost in love.
　　　But you'll say what you want to put her down,
　　　snarl like a monster, giggle like a clown.

Translated by Roz Kaveney

107　　When something happens you wanted and
　　　　　never hoped for
　　　That is, in the exact sense, a pleasure to the
　　　　　mind.
　　　And so to me it is a pleasure more precious
　　　　　than gold
　　　That you, Lesbia, return to me who desire you,
　　　Desire but have given up hoping; give yourself
　　　　　back
　　　To me: it is a day for a whiter mark.
　　　What man alive is happier than I, or could say
　　　There is anything more to be desired in this
　　　　　life?

Translated by C. H. Sisson

109 (You Promise Me My Love That This
Our Love)

The poet prays for length of love.

In one of her ribald moments she gave me a
    holy medal.
"Never has it been heard that a prisoner of war
    wearing
this badge of salvation has been executed."
O adorable Face.
Pray for my enemy.

Translated by Anne Carson

109   My life, my love, you say our love will last
          forever;
    O gods remember
    her pledge, convert the words of her avowal
          into a prophecy.
    Now let her blood speak, let sincerity govern
          each syllable fallen
    from her lips, so that the long years of our lives
          shall be
    a contract of true love inviolate
    against time itself, a symbol of eternity.

Translated by Horace Gregory

PERMISSIONS AND SOURCES